Thirteen Breaths To Freedom

An Introduction to Breathwork

James Beard

Sacred Systems
San Diego, CA

ISBN number 978-0-983-38140-2

Printed in the United States of America by Createspace

The intention of this writing is to share a Breathwork exercise I found helpful in my life. It is not my intention to replace medical care or give medical or psychological advice. I, the author and publisher and distributors, will not and cannot be held accountable for prosecution for any loss or harm, be it physical, mental or emotional, do to the material and intentions within this book.

Peace

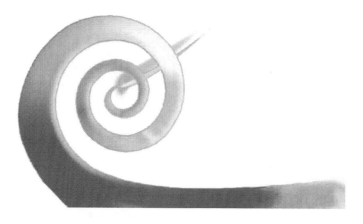

The spiral is a piece of my art inspired by this breathing exercise. It is one of many gifts that have come to life from within me during my Breathwork practice.

Gratitude

I am very grateful to Molly Zimmerman, for her patience, persistence and fierce honesty with my writing. Without her assistance, questions, and suggestions this book would not have the clarity it has today. Molly, thank you for the time and energy you put into this writing.

I am also thankful to, Maria Onofrietti, Dana Webster, Christine Cox, Bob Valentine, Sharri Gaines and Stephanie Armijo for their suggestions and timely bits of wisdom and insight.

Thank you mom, for your listening ear and watchful eye as this book came to completion. Dad, I miss you and I believe I felt your hand on my left shoulder many times as I read this writing out loud, to myself, sitting in your old chair.

I am also grateful to my daughters, Noelle and Megan, for supporting me in my Breathwork practice over the years.

Most of all I would like to thank the breath, the air we breathe and share, for touching me in ways that have been more fulfilling and astonishing than anything else I know.

Breathe

The Breath is the Vital Force
that sustains our life
as we know it
now

With that in mind
being able to direct
this force
is a key to unlocking
our full potential

Thirteen Breaths to Freedom

Foreword

Breathwork is the most powerful and well-rounded exercise I have practiced. It is healthy for my body, mind, and heart. It is one of the most influential and amazing experiences of my life, one of those peak experiences that never ceases to amaze me.

The profound awakenings and healings I see in my clients and in my personal practice leave me feeling invigorated, inspired and wanting to share Breathwork with everyone I know.

The purpose of this book is to shine a light on Breathwork, defining the word, and teaching the exercise, creating an avenue for you to experience Breathwork for yourself.

It is about a breathing exercise I created for myself, from which I have experienced many phenomenal benefits. I use it to uplift my spirit, to heal my body, and have a deeper spiritual understanding of my life. I believe the breathing exercises within this book can do the same for you.

Of all the metaphysical, new age, holistic, alternative healing, martial arts, yoga, and spiritual practices I have undertook, Breathwork is by far the best I have found. It can complement any of the above practices making them more effective, with quicker results and a deeper understanding of the practice.

The following pages contain part of my story, and how to apply the breathing exercises. It includes some pros and cons of Breathwork and thirteen different breathing exercises. The exercises are written in a *How To* format and laid out in a sequence that builds from one to the next, giving you an opportunity to create a strong foundation before diving into the advanced breaths.

The healing and revelations I experienced using Breathwork have been so wonderful and insightful in my life that I would like to see Breathwork become a household name. Something you would recommend to a friend just because it feels good.

Sometimes, when I talk about Breathwork, I feel like a chiropractor in the 1950s, trying to convince people to try a chiropractic session. I receive unsure, questioning looks, disbelief, and comments like, "I know how to breathe."

The material in this book is merely a suggestion of practicing a breathing exercise I created for myself. Is it right for you? Is it wrong for you? I don't know. What I do know is it works for me and many others so well, that I have been inspired to write it down.

I hope you find Thirteen Breaths to Freedom to be inspiring, beneficial, and applicable in your life.

Part of My Story

Childhood

As a young child I entertained myself with my breath in the latter years of elementary school. It was very interesting to me that I could not live more than a minute or so without breathing. When class was boring or slow, I would take a deep breath and watch the classroom clock's second hand ticking away time, to see how long I could hold my breath. Each new day I would try to hold it in longer than the day before. Some days I would increase holding my breath by a couple of seconds and sometimes I stretched it five or ten seconds. Over time I was able to easily hold my breath between one and a half to two minutes. When that became boring I started timing my inhales and exhales. Within a short period of time, I lengthened my inhale to one minute and slowed my exhale doing my best to make them equal in length. And the next day of school when class became slow I would do it again trying to make them longer than the day before.

Now that I look back at this particular time of my life, I recognize I was doing advanced breathing exercises designed to clear and focus the mind. I can't say it helped me focus on the teacher's lessons, but it did help the day go by.

Adolescence

In my early teens I tried holding my breath to help me fall asleep. I thought if I held my breath long enough, I would pass out and sleep. It had the reverse effect and once again I began timing how long I could hold my breath late into the night, watching the second hand tick by. I was able to hold my breath just beyond two minutes at that time.

Later in my teens, around eighteen years old, I changed directions with my breathing games as I tried to fall asleep. I did my best to breathe as little as possible, to completely let go of the breath as I relaxed and visualized my body with my mind. Over time I was able to relax my body on command. I could relax my body to sleep and listen to it quietly snore as I lied there consciously awake wondering where I went when my body was asleep.

One night as I was witnessing my body sleeping, my consciousness went blank for a split second. The next thing I knew I was looking down from my bedroom ceiling at the outline of my sleeping body under the covers with only my head sticking out. It was a shocking experience to say the least, but overall it was a defining moment in my life. That experience became the beginning of a quest to understand my life and the human potential. I had an out of body experience.

Young Adult

It was in the mid 1980s when I started doing specific breathing exercises and techniques to better understand myself. I practiced four-two breathing; counting to four on the inhale, holding the breath in for a count of two, exhaling for a count of four, and holding the breath out for a count of two. Then I repeated the exercise for several minutes. I also did six-three, eight-four breaths and Nadi Shodhana (right and left nostril breathing,) alternating inhales and exhales between the nostrils. Nadi Shodhana has been written about in many books that I have studied. I have also practiced it in many yoga classes without benefit of an explanation. I will share a purpose behind this breathing exercise now.

Nadi Shodhana is designed to help you balance the breath between your right and left nostrils while inhaling and exhaling. If you take the time right now to seal one nostril then the other and note the difference between the two, you may find one breathes easier than the other.

Nadi Shodhana is done in the following manner. Completely exhale while placing your index and middle finger of your right hand in between your eyebrows. Press your thumb on to the right side of your nose sealing the right nostril. Inhale completely through your left nostril, and then press your right ring finger and pinky on the left side of your nose sealing the left nostril while releasing your thumb from the right side and exhale. Now inhale through you right nostril completely then seal it and release your left nostril and exhale. This action is repeated for a designated amount of time or a number of 'rounds'. Besides the physical aspects of this particular breathing exercise, it is also done to balance the right and left Nadis (energy lines) that weave back and forth through the Chakra system located along the spine.

The Chakra system traditionally has seven main centers located from the base of the spine to the top of the head. The Chakras are described as energy centers within the body that have certain frequencies related to your emotions and organs. For a simple example, the first Chakra is associated with security (fight or flight) found at the base of the spine. The second Chakra ties to your sexuality and creativeness near the sacrum. The third Chakra relates to how we fit in the world and it is tied to the solar plexus. The fourth Chakra is the center of love located behind the sternum, known as the heart Chakra. The fifth is about expression found in the throat. The sixth is known as the third eye (all seeing) centered behind the eye brows and the seventh Chakra is tied to our spirituality and the crown of the head.

The right and left Nadis are called the Pingala and Ida. The Pingala Nadi is described as the solar or hot Nadi originating on the right side of the body. The Ida is associated with the moon or coolness and the left side of the body. This is where the Nadi Shodhana exercise becomes more esoteric and subtle. When you balance the Pingala and Ida Nadis another Nadi known as the Sushumna has the potential to open.

The Sushumna releases Kundalini energy up the spine through the main Chakra System from the base to the Crown Chakra. Kundalini is a hidden dormant energy residing within your first Chakra. This was an original idea behind balancing the breath between the right and left nostrils. It is an ancient, almost forgotten practice for pursuing enlightenment. Enlightenment is the ultimate goal of this practice and the energy of Kundalini, this hidden force within us, is a key, if not *the* key to a successful Nadi Shodhana practice.

During this time I also did breathing exercises that included visualizations designed to open the Chakras and release my Kundalini. I didn't experience much from these exercises except for stress reduction and a higher level of concentration. It didn't discourage me from pursuing enlightenment. Yes, I was pursuing enlightenment. I admit it; I wanted to know firsthand. I wanted the experience, the absolute truth. I wanted enlightenment and all the gifts that came with it. As the saying goes, "Be careful what you ask for." Now to continue with part of my story.

It wasn't until I took a workshop in 1992, which focused on the breath as a means of empowering myself, that I truly began to experience the power of the breath and the human potential. This was my introduction to Breathwork. It was in this weekend long workshop that I became empowered and awakened to a new reality, a new definition of life, a reality of love, unconditional love.

I signed up for this particular workshop not really knowing what I was getting into. I just trusted the enthusiastic person that suggested it and I was at a point in my life where I was ready for the depth of the Breathwork experience that I had.

Going through the process of that workshop, with every bit of my being, desire and concentration, took me further than I have ever been in my human experience to date. I released so much emotional baggage that some people in my life didn't even recognize me.

At the end of the workshop the facilitator told us not to do Breathwork on our own and that spoke directly to the rebel in me. I continued practicing and perfecting Breathwork for myself, leading me to the development of *Thirteen Breaths to Freedom*. I am capable of empowering myself with only thirteen breaths as described in this book and a portion of my workshop.

There is much more to my story and experience but this little book has been written to support and/or promote you having a personal Breathwork experience. You may find it reduces your stress levels too, calming your mind and relaxing your body or Breathwork may take you on your very own journey to a deeper understanding of your life; who and what you are. There is only one way to find out, and that is to try it for yourself.

Take a breath!

I wish you the best.

Guidance

I suggest you read this material straight through to the end before you begin practicing this exercise. Thirteen Breaths to Freedom is designed with the intention to take the reader from the first slow grounded breath, which lays out a foundation that builds up to the last fast intense breath, leaving one feeling ultimately free, light and loved.

The following thirteen breaths are exercises for those seeking to understand themselves, support a healthy lifestyle and deepen their spiritual practice. I suggest you work with the first breath until you are comfortable with it, because it leads to the second breath, and the second to the third, and so on. It may take a couple of days or it may take months or even years to become accomplished in Breathwork. On the other hand the breaths do not need to be practiced in the order they are presented and one breath can be worked on at a time.

There are four physical styles of breathing, with three breaths to each style and thirteen mental, emotional, and spiritual intentions within this Breathwork exercise. There is not a correct or incorrect way to do Breathwork, but there is a more productive way as previously mentioned. I will leave that for you to decide.

This is a powerful exercise so be mindful when doing *your* Breathwork practice. The Breathwork exercise is done lying down. You will find you can relax deeper lying on your back and you may fall asleep but that is better than falling out of a chair or getting a stiff neck. Reading this material to the end will help you see the bigger picture and full potential of this Breathwork exercise.

The first three breaths lay out the foundation of this practice. The second three breaths deepen and strengthen the foundation, while the third three breaths begin to build on it. The tenth breath is the sum total of the first nine breaths, whereas the eleventh breath extends out into the world. The twelfth breath is the essence within all the breaths and the last and final breath, the thirteenth, is the all-encompassing breath of life.

Here are thirteen suggestions for practicing the breathing exercises:

1. You can do the breaths as presented in this book.
2. You can work on the physical parts of the breathing.
3. You can work on the mental part.
4. You can work on the emotional part.
5. You can work on the first breath until you feel comfortable with it and then move on to the second breath and so on.
6. You can pick the breath you like most and work with it.
7. You can begin to memorize each breath in the order presented.
8. You can use one intention (I love myself) and physically breathe through the thirteen breaths to the hold.
9. You can add your own intention.
10. You can do it in silence.
11. You can add your favorite soundtrack, but remember to be mindful of the music you choose.
12. You can create a space and time specifically for your Breathwork practice.
13. You can do it with loving, supporting friends in a group.

Side Effects

The side effects, both positive and negative, range from pure bliss to Tetany. Tetany is basically a cramped muscle and bliss is an extraordinary sense of freedom. Tetany may show up in your breathing practice as a cramping of your hands or feet. If this happens, simply let your breathing resume to normal and open your eyes or you can go with it and realize something is happening on an energetic level. Remember there are three aspects of yourself involved; your body, your mind, and your heart, (your emotional self.)

For years, I only pitched the positive aspects of Breathwork so people would attend my private or group sessions. I noticed that some of the people that showed up, came with preconceptions of the experience they might have. I only told them about the positive benefits of Breathwork I experienced. I didn't tell them about the dark path I had to go down to get there. This *surprise* sometimes stopped them from going any further.

This is why I have written this section. I have heard both extremes, and that some of the Yogic breathing exercises, can make me crazy. Maybe they have and that is why I have decided to write this book. My truth is

Breathwork has helped answer a lot of my life's questions and empowered me to get on with living my life.

I have listed the following effects in two columns, pros and cons. You will notice some of the effects are in both columns. I actually feel all of the effects can have a positive spin on them. It may not feel good becoming dizzy, nauseous or going into Tetany, but those effects are letting me know something is happening within my body, mind, and spirit. I see that as an opportunity to work on myself. To me those are signs something within me is out of balance.

I recommend that you consult your medical advisor if you experience any of the cons before you explore Breathwork any further. On that same note you may want to let a good friend know if you have experienced any of the pros.

Breathwork, conscious breathing, is not some foolish new age movement. It is an exercise that has been practiced by Yogis and Traditional Chinese Medicine for thousands of years. It is a very powerful exercise that requires respect and discipline. Be very mindful while practicing this exercise and let people you trust know what you are about to embark upon. It can be quite a life changing experience.

Pros	Cons
Stress Reduction	Anxiety
Physical Healing	Dizziness
Emotional Healing	Nausea
Empowerment	Tetany
Heightened Senses	Headache
Revealed Inner Gifts	Changing
Spiritual Understanding	Facing Yourself
Intuition	Accepting Responsibility
Tetany	Revealing emotional wounds
Facing Yourself	
Changing	
Accepting Responsibility	
State of Oneness	
Dizziness	
Nausea	
Detoxifying	
Forgiveness	
Tingling	
Smiling	
Freedom	
Happiness	
Joy	

1

I Love My Body

I Love My Body

This is the first breath, of *Thirteen Breaths to Freedom*. It is the slowest of the thirteen breaths bringing your awareness to your breath moving within your body. The intentions are grounding, body awareness, and love.

There are many ways to love your body and doing Breathwork is one of them. The point of the statement, *I Love My Body* is to start a loving relationship with your body using the breath, your life force. If you can easily and honestly say, *I Love My Body* without any doubt, then you are in harmony with your body, mind, and spirit.

Most of us know how to love our bodies but do we do it? Do we eat nutritious food? Do we exercise regularly? Do we get enough rest? Do we nurture and pamper our bodies? Do we keep good company? Do we accept ourselves as we are? Do we keep all that in balance?

Just try saying the words *I Love My Body* out loud and see how you feel. Now try saying it with emotion, with a smile on your face. Now notice your body. Does it feel different? Were you able to say the words without hesitation, without doubt?

As you breathe in this higher vibration of love and empower it with the breath, you are creating the potential to reveal all that is not loving within you: Thoughts, memories and feelings from within your subconscious, may rise to the surface of your conscious mind, giving you a moment to see them in a new light and understanding, an opportunity to heal. Breathing these conscious breaths can be a very healing experience, clearing your body of negative energy. The intention of this breath is to help you find the origin, the roots of not loving your body so it can be forgiven and released.

If you already love your body then the potential of this Breathwork exercise may help you reveal your true essence, taking the love you have for your body to a new level of being.

The Breathwork exercise is done in the following manner. While holding the intention, *I Love My Body* in mind and breath, exhale completely, and then inhale this first, full, complete, breath slowly through your nose. As you slowly inhale through your nose, direct your awareness of your breath, down your back. Feel it expanding down your back like a light caress on the inside of your body all the way to the top of your hips. Now fill in the hip basin, with the sensation of inhaling, relaxing and opening as it goes further down to your perineum. (The perineum is the area between your sexual organ and your anus. This is a key area to relax and lovingly breathe into.) Then inhale on around and up your pelvis, soften and expand your belly. Move the breath on up through your heart center opening up the chest and throat completing the first slow inhale. This breath is massaging your organs and stretching your body from the inside out.

The exhale is naturally released by relaxing the chest and belly. Near the end of the exhale slowly contract your abs, your stomach and then your chest to squeeze out more air preparing your body for the next inhale. With the front of your body consciously engaged and contracted you will find it is easier to slowly direct your awareness of this breath down your back.

Your intention and feeling within this breath is love of your body. This is the thought and sensation you have within all thirteen breaths. When you align your body with love, you have the potential to take your physical experience to another level of being, extraordinary.

If you find you don't love your body, start with one part of your body and work on that learning to accept and love your body as it is now. Do your best to get to the core of it, where it originated and breathe it out of you. It is your divine birthright to feel loved and it is worth every breath.

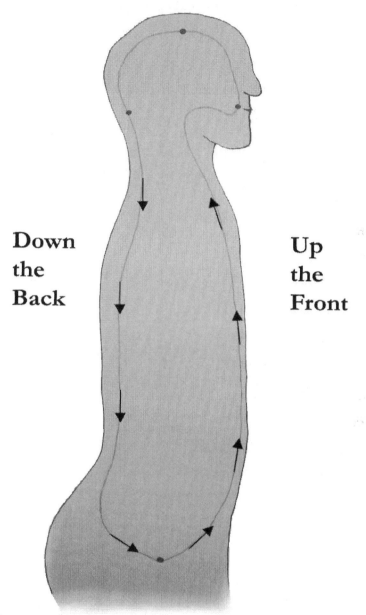

Down the Back

Up the Front

Around Through the Perineum

2

I Love My Mind

I Love My Mind

This is the second breath. Its intention is clarity and focus bringing our attention to our mind, the intender, the imaginative co-creator.

There are many ways to love our mind, doing Breathwork is definitely one of them. But the point of the statement, *I Love My Mind,* is once again, to energize the love of our thoughts, with our life force energy, the conscious breath. If you can easily and honestly say, *I Love My Mind*, without any doubt then you are very well off and in harmony with your mind and spirit.

Most of us know how to love our minds but do we do it? Do we meditate? Do we train our mind? Do we feed our minds good stories? Do we get enough rest? Do we keep our mind focused? Do we keep it present or allow it to wonder back into the past? Do we daydream? Do we keep all that in balance with our daily activities?

Saying the words, *I Love My Mind,* may be easier than, *I Love My Body*, because the mind is quick to change. But say it out loud out and see how you feel. Now say it with emotion, with a smile on your face, notice your mind. Is it clearer? Is it more present?

The intention of this breath is to recognize the power of our thoughts and the mind itself. In these breathing exercises your mind is involved in manipulating your breath in a way that is not natural to you at this time. Most of us breathe without thought of our breath. We take our breath for granted and it is one of the most powerful aspects of being human. Our breath is what gives us the ability to speak and the ability to pause, to breathe before speaking. Take a breath.

This is the second breath of Thirteen Breaths to Freedom. *I Love My Mind.* Breathe it in. Exhale completely and slowly inhale the same way as the first breath. Inhale through your nose, down your back, stretching all the way into your hip basin, relaxing and expanding as it moves down and on around up past your pelvis, softening and filling your belly, moving the breath up through your heart filling up your chest and throat.

Naturally release the breath allowing the chest and stomach to deflate with help at the end of the exhale to squeeze out more air. This engages the front of your body and prepares you for the next slow inhale that stretches and expands your body and mind. Keep the mind engaged with the intention, *I Love My Mind,* and let it become the witness as you breathe this circular, rhythmic breath.

3

I Love My Heart

I Love My Heart

This is the third breath. Its intention is love, bringing our awareness to our emotional self and our energetic heart, the center of our being, of love itself.

Opening your heart and allowing the expression of unconditional love to move through your body and mind from the depth, the core of your essence, can be, and is, a life-altering experience. Breathwork is a powerful exercise that has the potential and capability to do this. Doing Breathwork is one of the most direct ways to open up your heart and your emotional body, your loving self. This may take time, patience, kindness and gentleness as you stir up the painful pieces (anger, hate, resentment, sadness, fear, jealousy, guilt...) of your subconscious that have masked and hidden the innocence of your heart. These are core issues, defining moments in your life, definitions of yourself, as you know yourself now.

First you need to acknowledge you have a heart and be willing to do the work, to look at, and feel the scars and bruises of your past that have left you emotionally crippled. The things that were done to you and the things you did to others that have not been forgiven and released. Your heart is where your first layer of protection and self-preservation resides, the protective barriers of your past. They are the deepest of wounds where your innocence has been buried.

When digging up these old and deep wounds you need to create a safe and trusting space, a place where you can get to the root of the cause, that sealed your heart in the first place. In this time of your healing and forgiving you may feel vulnerable and unstable as the core pieces of your identity, your ego, begin to change, soften and love once again.

For some people just asking them to use the word, *Love,* is too much. Try it though in the secrecy of your home or your parked, engine off, none moving car with no one else around (Do not do any of these exercises while driving). If you made it that far, now try it with feeling and emotion, whatever that emotion and feeling may be within this moment. Let it out, scream it to the stars or into your pillow if you need to, but let it out, the present feeling, whatever it is, to make room for love.

Go ahead and try it. Now notice your body. Does it feel different? Can you laugh a little at the silliness and yet the power of it? When you can, when you feel that bubble of joy rising within you again, you will know first hand this work is worth doing. This is only the third breath of

Thirteen Breaths to Freedom. Breathe it in. *I Love My Heart.*

This breath is inhaled the same way as the first two but it is the last slow breath inhaled in through the nose completing the foundation, the stable rock, of this breathing exercise. Slowly breathe down your back with awareness through the back of your heart, into your hip basin expanding down to your perineum. Bring it on around and up to your pelvis, softening your belly, moving the breath up through the front of your heart, filling up your chest and throat with the intention and feeling of love.

Exhale relaxing and deflating your chest and belly while releasing the emotional residue of your past. Near the end of the exhale slowly contract and engage your chest and abs to squeeze out more air and emotion preparing your body, mind and heart for the next energetic inhale of life-force energy charged with love. With the front of your body contracted you will find it easier to slowly direct your awareness of the breath, the life-force energy, down your back stretching your body, mind and heart from the inside out.

Your intention while breathing this breath is love, love for yourself, for your being. This is the thought and feeling within all the breaths. Forgiveness and letting go are keys to becoming free. They're a grand part of this practice, releasing the energy of your past from your present, so you can live more fully and intuitively in this moment, your life.

4

My Body Is Relaxed

My Body Is Relaxed

This is the fourth breath. Its intention is relaxation, commanding your body's innate intelligence to relax itself.

This is where you learn to relax your body deeply with body awareness. In yoga this practice is called Savasana, corpse pose, or the dead man's pose. It is done lying down on your back on your yoga mat at the end of a yoga class. With this breath's intention relax every part of your body except for what it takes to breathe this circular breath. I recommend lying down as mentioned in the guidance section but it can be done in a seated position to keep you from falling asleep until you have more experience with relaxing your body while staying alert.

So how do we relax?

Here is an example: make a fist, squeeze it tight and then let it go. Now open your hand wide splaying and flexing the thumb and fingers out and back, and then let them go. You have just relaxed your flexors and extensors, opposing muscle groups that balance the action of your hand, the ability to hold on and let go.

Engage and release the muscles within the rest of your body. It is amazing what we hold unconsciously in our body, the unnecessary tension. It is time to find it and let it go. Curl your toes under and feel the muscles involved. Now lift your toes and feel the active muscles and then release them, feeling your feet, ankles, and calves relax. Bring your awareness up your leg, isometrically engage your thighs and buttocks contracting the opposing muscle groups in your upper leg and then release and relax your legs. Squeeze the muscles in your arms and shoulders, back and torso, and then let them go. Do this until your entire body is relaxed. Key areas to focus on are your hands, feet, hips and shoulders. Scan your body for tension and relax it. Soften and rest your closed eyes and relax your jaw, this quickens and deepens the relaxation process.

The ability to relax is crucial to reaching freedom. With time, like all exercises, it will become easier and the results quicker. You will soon be able to relax on command when your body awareness improves and your levels of relaxation deepen.

You may begin to sense your energetic body in this relaxed state of being. It is in this relaxed state that you can release your body's negative energy stored within your body's cellular memory, negative memories stored within your muscles, bones and nervous system that are no longer serving the life you desire. Cellular and muscle memory is another layer of your human experience that can be negative or positive. It is why you don't have to think about walking, talking, or reaching for a light switch. It is also why you may react in life, repeating actions, instead of pausing, taking a breath and acting in the moment.

My Body is Relaxed. Breathe it in. Keep your body tension free except for what it takes to breathe. Breathe in at a normal pace through your mouth with *a relaxed jaw* and then the same as before: breathe down your back, into your hip basin, relaxing and expanding as it goes down through your perineum, then on around and up to your pubic bone, beginning to soften and round your belly up to and through your heart, filling up the chest and throat. These exaggerated inhales and exhales are massaging your internal organs by stretching and squeezing them. The inhale is bringing in new life and the exhale is releasing the old.

The exhale is a natural release of the full inhale making a slight, *Ha,* like sound, like a quiet sigh. Once again engage the front of your body at the end of the exhale to squeeze out more air to prepare you for your next inhale. Keep your mind engaged and body relaxed with your intention and become aware of the new energy beginning to flow throughout your body.

Breathe

5

My Mind Is At Peace

My Mind Is At Peace

In the fifth breath of Thirteen Breaths to Freedom, you are intending mental peace while keeping your intentions in check and your body relaxed. At this point hopefully you have made peace with the four previous statements.

I love my body.
I love my mind.
I love my heart.
My body is relaxed.

The intention of, *My Mind Is At Peace* is to create the essence of peace, the feeling of tranquility. It is at this point in the breathing exercise that you do your best, to let go of the issues that may have been brought to the surface of your mind. Do this by focusing on the breath and the intention of peace, the feeling itself.

There is a memory within you somewhere when your mind was at peace, when your mind was free, clear and content. See if you can recall that peacefulness now. Breathe consciously, focusing on the feeling of serenity, tranquility and innocence. This is an act of being still in your body and your mind.

The fifth complete breath, like the fourth, is inhaled through your relaxed mouth. Lick your lips if necessary and do whatever it takes to keep your body comfortable. The peace in your mind helps your body relax even deeper. Breathe down your back, into your hip basin, all the way to your perineum, relaxing and expanding as it goes down around and up, releasing your belly, then up through your heart filling up your chest and throat with the feeling of peace.

The exhale is a natural release of the full inhale making a peaceful *Ha* like sound, like a calm sigh. Once again bring your attention to the front of your body at the end of the exhale to squeeze out a little bit more air to prepare you for your next inhale. Keep your mind peaceful and body relaxed with your intentions and become aware of the calm energy and peace beginning to flow throughout you.

6

My Heart Is Open

My Heart Is Open

In the sixth breath with our bodies relaxed and our minds at peace, our hearts can easily open.

My heart is open. What does that mean? Here is where we become somewhat esoteric. When we open our hearts, (our fourth chakra, Anahata) in an energetic sense, these are the attributes that come forth; acceptance, patience, kindness, gentleness, the adjectives of love, not only for others but for our self too.

One of the goals of Breathwork is opening yourself up so you are able to receive and give love. It is about healing the experiences in life, which have hardened us. The sixth breath is bringing awareness to and of your heart center. It is reinforcing the intention of the third breath, *I Love My Heart.*

As we begin this new relationship with our body, mind and heart, we will discover our heart is not just an organ pumping blood throughout our body but an energy center of love, the very essence of what we are.

In this sixth breath, the breath is inhaled the same way as the fourth and fifth. Beginning at the end of your exhale, inhale a full breath through your relaxed mouth and peaceful mind opening your heart to a new way of being.

The six breath is the same as the fourth and the fifth. Breathe the life-force energy into and through your relaxed mouth and down your spine. Breathe all the way down to the tip of your tail bone, stretching and expanding as you guide the breath further down through your perineum. Breathe on across and up front of your body, softening your belly, opening your heart, filling up your chest and throat with love.

The exhale is a natural release of the full inhale making a calm *Ha* sound, like a gentle release. Once again soothingly engage the front of the body at the end of the exhale to squeeze out more air to prepare your body for your next inhale. Keep your mind engaged and body relaxed with the intention, *My Heart Is Open,* and become aware of the energy of love beginning to flow throughout your being.

7

I Am Alive

I Am Alive

The seventh breath's intention is life; it is about recognizing your life as a gift, challenging as it is. This gift, human life, has many lessons and experiences to suffer and enjoy. Since you are reading this I can only assume you are looking to get more out of your life. If you have the answers and are at peace with the following questions then you are ahead of the game and possibly ready to take your life to a new level of experience. If not, then that is the intention of this breath.

- ❏ I am alive. What does that mean?
- ❏ Why am I here?
- ❏ Why am I alive?
- ❏ Why was I born into this family?
- ❏ Is there a purpose to my life?
- ❏ Is there an honest answer to these questions?

Many people and organizations claim to have an answer to those questions. It's big business. Religion, healthcare, self-help, psychology, psychiatry, drugs, alcohol, and sex all claim to have an answer of some sort and they do. But are the answers complete? Are they absolute truth? Do they satisfy, leaving you feeling content and free?

Breathwork, on the other hand, is designed to help you help yourself and bring forth the answers from within. It compliments any of the above, because you can apply it to their intention. Breathwork is a combination of knowledge and experience and that creates wisdom. While breathing in the intention of this portion of the Breathwork exercise, ask yourself some of the questions above or ask yourself if you are truly living. Are you living your full potential?

Hopefully at this point you are comfortable with the six previous Breathwork intentions so you can really begin to let yourself go. This breath is where you start to go for it, where you start to live and remember your calling.

In the seventh breath, *I Am Alive*, you begin to breathe through your mouth like you are breathing through a big smoothie straw. Exhale completely, purse your lips, so when you inhale you hear the air move across your lips and teeth. Now breathe new life into your body, mind, and heart. At this point in this Breathwork exercise breathe as completely as you can without being too mental about the process, trust the foundation you have established. *Feel* your breath move down the back of your body, feel the expansion and softening of your perineum, feel your belly rise before your heart and chest and exhale with a *Ha* sound.

Remember your intention, *I Am Alive*, (I am here, I have a purpose, etc.) and breathe it in with feeling and clarity. Exhale out the stale dull pieces of your past still lingering around inside of you. Squeeze out a little bit more of your past engaging the front of your body in the present moment, to prepare you for the next inhale, the next inspiration of your life.

Breathe

8

I Am Focused

I Am Focused

The eighth breath, *I Am Focused,* pretty much speaks for itself. Breathwork is a powerful exercise that has the potential to change your inner landscape. So being focused is crucial while empowering the breath, the life force energy, with your intention and emotion.

The overall focus of these breathing exercises is love, love for and of yourself. When you breathe in, *I Am Focused*, it is not so much the words you are saying, as it is the feelings you are feeling and the amount of clarity you have about the thirteen Breathwork intentions.

So the intention of the eighth breath becomes a form of *protection* by keeping your mind focused on the Breathwork exercise and the overall theme, love. This is not a time to let your mind wander. Your focused intention is capable of penetrating the un-serving layers of your life, allowing your heart to open in a safe way. This breathing exercise is where you really begin to let your outer self go and let your inner self shine through. Keeping your mind focused and present on the thirteen intentions protects you from a random thought becoming energized by the breath and established within you.

One of my teachers once told me, "Be careful what you take in there with you." Breathwork is capable of bringing these intentions, your thoughts, to life. Be very mindful when doing your practice. Create a safe and quiet space, for your Breathwork sessions, with enough time at the end to gather yourself up, before facing the outside world. As you begin to deepen your intentions with the breath, you will understand the importance of my teacher's statement above.

At the end of your exhale breathe in through your mouth like you are breathing through a big smoothie straw. This breath is the same as the seventh, purse your lips so when you inhale you hear the air move across your lips, teeth and tongue. This restrictive breath requires more energy and concentration. Focus on the breath moving down your back and up the front of your body. Do your best to keep your body relaxed as you breathe in as completely as you can and then exhale with a *Ha* sound. Help the end of the exhale by squeezing out a little more air controlling the front of your body. Remember your intention *I Am Focused* and breathe it in with feeling and meaning.

9

I Am Connected

I Am Connected

The ninth breath is about connection, a relationship with our self. It is about our relationship with everything. I am connected. What does that mean? A sense of belonging, yes, but let's go deeper than that to the unseen, the unheard, untouched connection that weaves through all of us. It is felt within you. It is a knowing, a sensation starting on the inside moving out. This connection is about the source that gives us life and how we are all part of this source. We are all one, only forgotten.

Breathing in the meaning and feeling, of the words *I Am Connected,* within this breath, are designed to stir up the memory and experience of oneness. Breathe it in and breathe out that which no longer serves. Begin to recognize your connection to oneness, to everything. The breath is a great example of the invisible energy, a connection we all share.

We are all one, fragmented and separated into personal experiences. We are life itself experiencing it through the five human senses. Our connection to the One is our connection to everything.

The focus of the ninth breath is dissolving the ego, your personal identity and allowing your heart to open, dissolving the boundary of your body and mind, which separates you from connecting to the unwavering unconditional love, supporting and sustaining everything. Opening your heart will give you the ability to love life unconditionally. This part of the breathing exercise is where we really begin to let your inner self shine through.

Once again breathe through your mouth like you are breathing through a big smoothie straw. Purse your lips so when you inhale you hear the air move across your teeth and tongue. This restrictive breath generates more energy and focus while inhaling this way. Do your best to keep your body relaxed and mind focused as you breathe as completely as you can. Feel the connection of your breath moving through and down your torso and back up through your heart, weaving your body, mind, and heart into harmonious wholeness. Exhale a healthy sigh, emptying out the lungs, squeezing out a little more air preparing you for the next inhale. Remember your intention and the meaning of, *I Am Connected*, and breathe it in with the desire to know firsthand that you are part of everything. Believe in and trust yourself.

10

I Love Myself

I Love Myself

This is the tenth breath. Its intention is love. I have found in my workshops and private sessions this is hard for some people to say, let alone do.

Saying these three words, *I Love Myself*, can stir the waters of your soul and charging them with the breath can be a very powerful experience. If you are in true alignment with these words, *I Love Myself*, the waters of your soul will remain calm and still, and reflect light. It is when they ripple and the reflection of your true essence is blurred and distorted, that we know our love is not pure.

If your inner pool is rippled that is a perfectly normal human experience. If you wish to see your pool calm and clear, let your inner work begin. Pick a ripple. What is it, about speaking these three words, *I Love Myself*, that ripples your inner pool of light? What comes to the surface? Words, images, sounds, colors, smells, feelings, memories…

Breathe! Take a breath.

When you lie down, close your eyes to the outside world and breathe, your subtle inner world will become more apparent and you will recognize how it reflects itself into your outer world, your perceptions and reactions.

Here is where it gets a little tricky. I don't want to project any ideas or expectations you may experience with Breathwork. I am here to simply remind you, that you are loved. To really understand and know this, begin by loving yourself.

I love myself.

What does that mean? It can be incredibly personal and it can be very simple.

Now here comes the fun. Let's define "I". What does "I" mean?

Play with that for a moment.

Now define "Love". What kind of love do you have for yourself? Is it puppy dog love or I would do anything for you love?

Now define "Myself". This is where you begin to recognize your multifaceted self, the total self, the light and the dark, the beautiful and ugly parts of your being, your many faces and gestures you show to the world.

"I" is the very beginning of defining your self in any given moment.

"Love" is a spectrum of feelings, thoughts, ideals, and connections in motion.

"Myself" is a body, a mind, an emotional heart, and spirit, filled with memories and dreams, the past and the future, and presently aware of both.

Love your multifaceted self through the spectrum of love, feel the connection both inside and outside of yourself.

In the tenth breath you breathe without thinking about it, letting yourself go, really letting your most central self shine through. Once again breathe through your mouth like you are breathing through a big smoothie straw. Purse your lips so when you inhale you hear and feel the life force energy move across your lips, teeth and tongue. This is a quick, full, powerful, breath, fill your lungs to their capacity as quickly as you can and then exhale, empty them just as quick and complete. The tenth breath is still restrictive and requires a lot of energy and concentration to inhale and exhale this way.

Do your best to keep your body relaxed as you quickly breathe in and breathe out. Exhale with a heavy *Ha* sound releasing your jaw and quickly inhale again. Remember your intention, *I Love Myself*, and breathe it in with passion and purpose, feel it, see it, imagine it, visualize it, know you are worthy of it. You are loved.

11

I Love My Life

I Love My Life

I love my life is another way of saying I love my co-creation. Your life is your creation within the group consciousness of all of us.

I love my life is just an extension of loving yourself. Loving your life is coming to peace with your past. I find forgiveness, to be a big part of loving yourself and your life. This is deep cellular and subconscious work. I use the word, *work* because it takes effort and that effort is worth every ounce of energy you use to discover the love within you.

Loving your life involves loving your family, your work (job, career, boss), your weekends, and dreams. To break this down into little details you can use some of the following phrases to see how you feel about them. *I love my dad. I love my mom. I love my job, my boss,* and so on. *I Love My Life*, my entire life, is not just picking and choosing what you like. It's lovingly accepting all the parts of your life, the obvious and the subtle, which identify or have identified who you are and what you have become.

In the eleventh breath, we continue the quick, full, powerful, passionate, breaths without thinking about it, to really let our inner nature stand out. Once again breathe through your mouth like you are breathing through a big smoothie straw. Pucker your lips so when you inhale you hear the breath stream across your pursed lips and teeth filling your body, mind, and soul with life.

This quick, full, powerful, breath is inhaled with passion. It is concentrated and directed, requiring a lot of energy and focus to inhale and exhale this way. Do your best to keep the rest of your body relaxed as you quickly breathe in and breathe out.

Exhale with a heavy *Ha* sound releasing your jaw and quickly inhale again. Remember your intention, *I Love My Life*, and breathe it in with confidence and expression.

12

I Am Love

I Am Love

Stating, *I Am Love,* is recognizing the very core of your being, *Love.*

Say it,

Feel it,

Know it,

Be it,

Love.

But remember where you are now and what world you are living in. This is about changing your inner world and then your outer world will follow. If this is the change you truly want, be prepared for your outer world to truly change.

What does this mean?

It means you may vibrate at a different level of energy than you do now and have in the past. You may no longer be in harmony with some of the people, places and things that are in your life now. This is a delicate time. If you reach your inner self, the light and unconditional love within you, you may have a hard time settling back into the life you were leading up until this moment. You will be self-empowered, enlightened, and the energetic games you played for energy will know longer be necessary because you have tapped into the source of all things. It may only last a moment, a day, a week, or months, or more. But in this altered state of being, be mindful of your decisions and actions as you adjust to the forgotten, loving energy settling within you.

In the twelfth breath, you continue the quick powerful breaths without putting too much thought into it. Allow yourself to sink deep within this breath letting your outside self go so your inner self can show itself to the outside world. Breathe through your mouth like you are breathing through a big smoothie straw. Purse your lips so when you inhale you hear the life force energy move into your body with passion and purpose.

This is a quick, full, powerful, breath. Do not underestimate its ability to rock your world. In its restrictiveness find the desire to pull the intention of this breath deep into your body. *I Am Love*. Feel the energy of it building within you. Do your best to keep the rest of your body at ease as you swiftly breathe in and breathe out. Exhale with a *Ha* sound and inhale again quickly. Remember your intention, *I Am Love*, breathe it in, be it. Be the feeling, the essence of love, let it shine throughout your being.

13

I Am

I Am

I Am is the thirteenth breath. It is a key to your being. *I Am*, is a spiritual seal of undeniable existence. Nobody ever told me about, *I Am* or that I am. The fact, that I exist, is that I am. We label ourselves beginning with *I am*, I am this, I am that. This is how we define ourselves be it what we do or how we feel. Examples: "Hi, I am James, I am a Breathworker." "I am happy." "I am sad." "Hi, I am so and so, I am a…" The truth is the more we add after the words, *I am*, the further away from source we have become, disconnected and separated in a sense of being. In the greater picture we are all one, it is the small definitions of *I Am* that we suffer and stress about our lives.

To sit within the eternal essence of *I Am* is to be immersed in the omniscient presence and power, of the substance, the heartbeat of life everywhere. The experience of those two little words is an extraordinary, life-altering occurrence, a pivotal turning point within your life. To breathe in the true spirit of *I Am* is to courageously breathe in self- worth, spiritual union and truth. To allow the *I Am Energy* to be absorbed throughout your being is courageous and bold. Once touched by this unconditional love and infinite light of *I Am* your life will never be the same. You will know first hand, all is perfect, and can be nothing less.

This is the thirteenth and final breath of this Breathwork exercise. You will continue the quick, powerful, inhale, breathing through your mouth like you are breathing through a big smoothie straw. Quickly fill your lungs to their capacity and then hold the inhale *in.* Hold your breath with the *I Am* intention focused in your mind, body, and heart, while relaxing the rest of your body except for what it takes to hold your breath.

Relax your perineum, while holding your breath for a few seconds or more and then release your breath with a natural exhale and no help at the end, *just let go.* Lie in this state without any effort from your mind or will, and let your body resume a natural breath. Enjoy your true self as it merges with your body, mind, and heart. Be a witness to your body's natural state. With practice and time you will feel the freedom of the thirteenth breath, *I Am.*

Thirteen Breaths to Freedom

I Love My Body

I Love My Mind

I Love My Heart

My Body Is Relaxed

My Mind Is At Peace

My Heart Is Open

I Am Alive

I Am Focused

I Am Connected

I Love Myself

I Love My Life

I Am Love

I AM

The light was so bright

I opened my eyes.

Author's Note

Now you know you can just breathe the first breath and receive fantastic benefits from that breath. Even without the first intention. Simply breathing a conscious breath can clear your mind and relax your body. It can stretch you from the inside out, massaging your heart, liver and other internal organs.

You now know adding an intention to your breath can increase the benefits and power of Breathwork and take it to another level. I have found it worthwhile to explore the more advanced levels of breathing, for a deeper understanding of myself, my life, and the life force energy that sustains them.

Thirteen Breaths to Freedom, my exercise, makes my life flow in more synchronistic ways. It aligns and sets my intention, my purpose in life, to be at the right place, at the right time, and in the right frame of mind. It has only been when I wasn't listening to the subtleness of my intuition, and not practicing this exercise that I would slip out of the synchronistic flow. In those moments I let the outside world have more of an influence on me than my inside world.

Once I notice I have slipped out of the flow, I use this breathing exercise as a reset button to realign my life and myself with the positive currents of life.

The breath is a great teacher of giving and receiving or taking and leaving. This little book is an exhale, of part of my experience with Breathwork. It is something for me to leave behind that you may breathe in. It is part of my giving back, for all the wonderful healing, and enlightening experiences I have received from Breathwork.

May you find…

what you seek.